Cooking vegetarian recipes can be a great way to introduce your kids to healthy eating habits and help them develop healthy lifestyle choices. Whether your family follows vegetarianism for ethical reasons, health reasons, or just to try something new, vegetarian recipes can be an excellent choice for kids.

Before you get started preparing vegetarian meals for the kids, there are some things you should take into consideration. First, make sure that the vegetarian recipes you choose are age-appropriate and safe for children to eat. You also want to make sure that the vegetarian meals contain enough nutrients and vitamins to maintain a healthy diet.

Once you've chosen vegetarian recipes suitable for kids, it is important to make sure that they are prepared correctly. Take the time to read through the recipe thoroughly and get all of the ingredients measured out, chopped up, and ready to go before you begin cooking. This will help reduce any confusion or mistakes during the process. It is also helpful to have your kids involved in meal preparation by having them help measure ingredients or stir a pot.

Finally, vegetarian recipes can be made even more fun and delicious by adding some creative touches such as colorful vegetables or unique spices. You can also incorporate vegetarian-friendly food items like tofu or tempeh into your recipes to add variety. With the right vegetarian recipes and preparation techniques, you can help your kids enjoy healthy vegetarian meals.

Tacos

Vegetarian tacos are a great way to introduce vegetarian recipes to kids. This vegetarian taco recipe is simple and delicious, using quick-pickled onions, creamy avocado dip, easy refried beans and 8 corn tortillas. To top it off, add some salsa verde, shredded green cabbage for extra crunch, fresh cilantro and lime wedges. These vegetarian tacos are healthy, tasty options that can easily be added to your family's meal rotation! Kids will love these vegetarian tacos - they're sure to become a favorite! Try this vegetarian taco recipe today and enjoy the yummy benefits of vegetarian cooking with your family!

To make vegetarian tacos, start by preparing the quick-pickled onions. Then, prepare the creamy avocado dip and easy refried beans. Warm up 8 corn tortillas in a pan over medium heat for about 15 seconds on each side. Fill each taco with a spoonful of refried beans and top them off with some salsa verde, shredded green cabbage, cilantro, and lime wedges. Enjoy vegetarian tacos - healthy recipes for kids that are sure to be a hit!

Vegetarian tacos are an easy way to incorporate vegetarian recipes into your family's meal rotation while still keeping everyone happy. With quick-pickled onions, creamy avocado dip, easy refried beans and warm corn tortillas, these vegetarian tacos are sure to be a hit with kids and adults alike. Enjoy vegetarian tacos for a healthy and delicious meal that your whole family will love!

Try this vegetarian taco recipe today and enjoy the yummy benefits of vegetarian cooking with your family! It's easy to make, healthy, and the perfect vegetarian recipes for kids. Start by preparing the quick-pickled onions, creamy avocado dip, and easy refried beans. Warm up 8 corn tortillas in a pan over medium heat for 15 seconds on each side. Toppings include salsa verde, shredded green cabbage, cilantro, and lime wedges. Serve vegetarian tacos as an easy way to get everyone excited about vegetarian meals!
Enjoy!

Lasagna

This vegetarian lasagna is a healthy and delicious meal that kids of all ages will enjoy! It's packed with nutritious vegetables, savory tomato sauce, and creamy white sauce. To make this dish, start by preheating your oven to 180°C/Gas Mark 4.

Next, prepare the vegetables: cut the red peppers into large chunks and slice the aubergines into ½ cm thick slices. Heat 8 tablespoons of olive oil in a large frying pan over medium heat and add the red pepper chunks and aubergine slices. Cook for 8-10 minutes until they are lightly browned.

In another pan, add 1 tablespoon of olive oil over medium heat and sauté the onions and garlic until soft. Add the carrot and tomato purée and cook for a few minutes. Pour in the wine and allow it to reduce by half before adding the canned tomatoes. Simmer for 20 minutes until you have a thick sauce. Finally, add the basil leaves and season with salt and pepper.

To make the white sauce, melt the butter in a pan over low heat. Add the flour and stir together until there are no lumps. Gradually add in the milk, stirring constantly until it forms a smooth sauce.

Now you're ready to assemble your vegetarian lasagna! Grease an oven-proof dish with olive oil and begin layering with lasagne sheets, vegetables, tomato sauce, white sauce, mozzarella cheese, and cherry tomatoes. Repeat until you have used all the ingredients and top with extra mozzarella cheese. Bake in the preheated oven for 30 minutes, or until golden brown on top.

This vegetarian lasagna is an easy-to-make dish that kids will love! The vegetables are full of healthy vitamins and minerals, while the tomato and white sauces add a wonderful depth of flavor. Serve it up with a side salad for a complete vegetarian meal that's sure to satisfy even the pickiest eaters. Bon appétit!

Greek Pasta Salad

Greek Pasta Salad is a vegetarian recipe that can be enjoyed by kids and adults alike. It's a healthy, vibrant dish with plenty of flavor to keep everyone happy! To make this delicious salad, start by boiling 12 ounces of mini farfalle pasta according to package instructions. Drain and set aside to cool. While the pasta is cooling, prepare the other ingredients: halve and pit 1/2 cup Kalamata olives; dice 1/3 cup red onion; cut 2 cups English or Persian cucumbers into half moons; halve 2 cups (1 pint) cherry tomatoes; dice 1 cup green bell pepper; chop 1/4 cup parsley; cube 1/2 cup feta cheese.

Once all the ingredients are ready, combine them in a large bowl. Add the cooled pasta, olives, red onion, cucumbers, tomatoes, bell pepper, parsley and feta cheese. Mix everything together until evenly combined. Serve chilled or at room temperature. Enjoy!

This vegetarian recipe is sure to be a hit with your kids. Not only is it healthy and full of flavor but it's also easy to make. You can prepare all the components ahead of time and let everyone customize their own bowl with their favorite ingredients. Greek Pasta Salad is perfect for lunchboxes or as part of a special weekend meal. Bon appétit!

Veggie Burritos

Preparing this vegetarian burrito recipe for kids is easy! Start by cooking the cilantro-lime rice according to package instructions. Meanwhile, heat a large skillet over medium-high heat and add oil. When hot, add black beans that have been seasoned with chipotle spice. Cook until heated through and beginning to char, stirring occasionally. Next, add peppers and onions to the pan and cook until softened, about 5 minutes more.

To make the avocado cream sauce, prepare it in a food processor by adding avocado, cilantro, jalapeño, garlic, lime juice and either sour cream or Greek yogurt. Process until fully combined before removing from heat and stirring in 3 Tbsp of water for desired consistency.

Once all components of the vegetarian burrito are ready, have kids help assemble their creation. This recipe is great for vegetarian recipes for kids and healthy recipes they can create themselves! Enjoy!

Ginger Sesame Noodles

Ginger sesame noodles is an easy vegetarian recipe that's perfect for kids. It's packed with flavor and is a healthy alternative to take-out noodles. To make this delicious dish, you will need 1/2 cup plus 2 tablespoons of low sodium soy sauce or tamari, 1/4 cup honey, 2 tablespoons balsamic vinegar, 2 tablespoons rice vinegar, 3 tablespoons creamy peanut butter or tahini, 1 tablespoon molasses or pomegranate molasses (optional), 2 tablespoons fresh grated ginger and 3 cloves garlic grated.

To begin preparing your ginger sesame noodles dish for your family dinner table, start by mixing together all the ingredients in a bowl until fully combined. Then pour the mixture into a pot, and heat until it comes to a boil. Reduce the heat and simmer for 10 minutes. Once cooked, transfer the noodles into a serving bowl and serve with your favorite vegetarian toppings such as diced tomatoes or avocado slices. Enjoy this vegetarian recipe that's perfect for kids!

Ginger sesame noodles is not only delicious but also healthy and easy to prepare. With the combination of fresh ingredients like honey, ginger and garlic, you can make sure that your family will be enjoying an irresistible meal in no time! Give this vegetarian recipe for kids a try and watch them finish their plates in seconds!

Homemade Veggie Dogs

Veggie dogs are a vegetarian alternative to traditional hot dogs, perfect for kids who don't eat meat or as an excuse to sneak in some extra veggies. Preparing veggie dogs at home is easy and healthy, using only simple ingredients like carrots, apple cider vinegar, tamari and seasonings. This recipe will give you vegetarian-friendly hot dogs that are sure to please even the pickiest of eaters.

To begin preparing the veggie dogs, start by preheating your oven to 350°F. Next, scrub 8 medium-sized carrots with a vegetable brush and slice them into "hot dog" shapes about 5 inches long and 1 inch thick. Place the carrot slices on a large baking pan lined with parchment paper and generously drizzle with avocado oil. Bake in the oven for 30 minutes, or until the carrots are tender.

While the carrots are baking, make the marinade by combining ¼ cup apple cider vinegar, ¼ cup tamari, 1 tablespoon smoked paprika and 1 teaspoon garlic powder in a medium bowl. Stir to combine and add 2-3 tablespoons of water if needed for a thinner consistency.

Once the carrots have finished baking, transfer them to a large bowl and pour the marinade over top. Toss gently to coat evenly and let sit for 15 minutes so that all the flavors can meld together. Serve vegetarian hot dogs on buns with your favorite toppings like ketchup, mustard or relish and enjoy!

Veggie dogs are a great vegetarian option for kids, offering a healthy alternative to traditional hot dogs. Packed with nutrients like vitamins A and C, these homemade veggie dogs are sure to be a hit with the whole family. With just a few simple steps, you can have delicious vegetarian recipes ready in no time – perfect for busy weeknight dinners or summer barbecues. Enjoy!

Pesto Quesadillas

If you're looking for vegetarian recipes for kids that are both healthy and delicious, try making these pesto quesadillas! Perfectly cheesy and packed with flavour, they'll become a family favourite in no time.

To make the pesto quesadillas, start by thinly slicing one roma tomato and gathering 3/4 cup of fresh baby spinach. Add 1/4 cup of vegan pesto to the vegetables; if desired, adjust this amount to suit your taste preferences. Next, add 1/2 cup of vegan mozzarella shreds (we recommend Follow Your Heart or Miyokos) as well as 1/4 cup of optional vegan feta crumbles. Place all of the ingredients onto two large tortillas (gluten-free if desired).

Once all of the ingredients are in place, carefully fold the tortillas over and press down to secure the ingredients. Preheat a skillet over medium heat and lightly grease with oil or vegan butter. Place the quesadilla onto the hot skillet and cook for 1-2 minutes on each side until golden brown. Finally, slice into wedges and serve warm!

Your vegetarian kids will love these delicious pesto quesadillas! Enjoy as a main dish, healthy lunchbox treat, or snack. Bon appetite!

Vegetable Pizza

Vegetarian pizza is a flavorful and healthy option for kids that's simple to prepare. There are so many vegetarian pizza toppings available, it's easy to create unique recipes that appeal to the whole family.

To make vegetarian pizza, start by preheating your oven according to the instructions on the package of store-bought or homemade pizza dough. Next, select your favorite vegetarian toppings. Tomatoes, onions, arugula, kale, eggplants, bell peppers, spinach, zucchini and mushrooms all make wonderful vegetarian topping choices. For even more flavor you can add in some cooked or roasted vegetables such as olives or artichoke hearts. Spread your selected toppings over the prepared crust and top with your desired amount of cheese.

Bake the vegetarian pizza in the oven according to the dough packaging instructions and enjoy! Vegetarian pizzas are a great way to provide kids with healthy vegetarian recipes that they can enjoy. Experiment with different types of vegetables, cheeses and seasonings to create vegetarian recipes for kids that everyone will love. With just a few simple steps you can have a delicious vegetarian pizza ready to eat in no time!

Vegan Caprese Pasta

12 OUNCES SPAGHETTI (GF IF
PREFERRED)
2 TABLESPOONS OLIVE OIL , EXTRA
VIRGIN.
¼ TEASPOON CRUSHED RED PEPPER
FLAKES (OPTIONAL)
3 CLOVES GARLIC , MINCED.
2 PINTS CHERRY TOMATOES , HALVED.
1 TEASPOON SEA SALT , MORE TO TASTE
(OR PREFERRED SALT)
FRESH CRACKED PEPPER , TO TASTE.

This vegetarian vegan caprese pasta is a great meal for kids of all ages. It's healthy and easy to prepare, so even the youngest chefs can help out! To make this delicious vegetarian recipe, start by bringing a pot of salted water to boil. Once boiling, add the spaghetti and cook according to package instructions until al dente.

While the spaghetti cooks, heat olive oil in a large skillet over medium-high heat. Add crushed red pepper flakes (if desired) garlic, cherry tomatoes, salt and pepper; stir frequently until vegetables are tender and fragrant.

Once the spaghetti is cooked, drain it and place it back into the pot; top with prepared vegetables and combine gently. Serve hot or chilled, with freshly grated Parmesan cheese if desired. Enjoy!

This vegetarian vegan caprese pasta is a great option for anyone looking to add a healthy and delicious meal to their weekly menu. It's also vegetarian, making it perfect for kids who are vegetarian or transitioning towards vegetarianism. With just a few ingredients and some basic cooking techniques, you can have this tasty dish ready in no time! So give it a try today and see how much your family loves it!

Crispy Potato Tacos

INGREDIENTS

2 LARGE RUSSET POTATOES.
¾ CUP SOUR CREAM.
2 CLOVES GARLIC, MINCED.
½ TEASPOON CUMIN.
SALT, TO TASTE.
½ TEASPOON OREGANO.
8 CORN TORTILLAS.
OIL, FOR FRYING.

Crispy potato tacos are a healthy vegetarian recipe for kids that is easy to prepare. Start by preheating your oven to 400°F and scrubbing the potatoes clean. Cut them into thin slices, about ¼-inch thick, and place onto a baking sheet lined with parchment paper. Drizzle with oil and sprinkle with salt, then bake for 25 minutes or until golden brown.

While the potatoes are baking, make the sour cream garlic sauce by combining the sour cream, minced garlic, cumin, oregano and salt in a bowl. Mix ingredients until everything is well combined.

Once the potatoes have finished baking, heat up some oil in a large skillet over high heat. Place four of the tortillas in the skillet and cook for 30-45 seconds per side until lightly browned. Place them on a plate lined with paper towels to absorb any excess oil.

To assemble tacos, place two potato slices inside each tortilla, then top with some of the sour cream garlic sauce and fold in half. Repeat this process with the remaining four tortillas and serve immediately. Enjoy!

These vegetarian crispy potato tacos are sure to be a hit amongst kids and adults alike! So next time you're looking for an easy, healthy vegetarian recipe for kids, try making these delicious tacos. They'll definitely make dinner time much more fun!

Pasta Primavera

INGREDIENTS
PENNE PASTA
SALT
OLIVE OIL
FRESH VEGGIES INCLUDING RED
ONION, CARROT, BROCCOLI, BELL
PEPPER, YELLOW SQUASH,
ZUCCHINI, TOMATOES AND GARLIC
2 TSP DRIED ITALIAN SEASONING
2 TBSP FRESH LEMON JUICE
2 TBSP CHOPPED FRESH PARSLEY
1/2 CUP SHREDDED PARMIGIANO,
DIVIDED

Pasta primavera is a vegetarian recipe for kids that's healthy, delicious, and full of fresh veggies. Preparing this recipe is easy and fun - all you need to do is gather the necessary ingredients (listed above) and get cooking!

To begin, cook penne pasta according to package instructions. Once cooked, drain pasta and set aside. Heat olive oil in a large skillet over medium heat. Add red onion and carrot; sauté until softened, about 5 minutes. Next add broccoli, bell pepper, yellow squash, zucchini, tomatoes and garlic. Season with salt and Italian seasoning; cook until vegetables are al dente - tender but still slightly crisp - about 5-7 minutes more.

Add cooked penne to skillet and mix to combine. Stir in lemon juice, parsley, and ¼ cup parmigiano cheese. Cook until cheese is melted and everything is combined. Taste for seasoning; add salt or Italian seasoning as needed. Remove from heat and serve pasta primavera with extra parmigiano on top. Enjoy!

This vegetarian pasta dish will be a hit with kids - it's healthy and loaded with flavor! Serve your family this delicious vegetarian recipe for an easy weeknight dinner that everyone will love. Bon Appetite!

Crispy Black Bean And Sweet Potato Tacos

Ingredients
8-10 tortillas (see notes)
2 14 oz can black beans, drained.
2 sweet potatoes, diced (skin on or peeled)
1 Tablespoon oil.
1/2 teaspoon (each) cumin, paprika, chili powder.
1/2 teaspoon garlic powder.
salt to taste.

These vegetarian black bean and sweet potato tacos are an easy, healthy, and delicious way to get your kids eating vegetarian! They can be made in under 30 minutes with very few ingredients - perfect for busy nights. To prepare, simply heat up the oil in a large skillet over medium-high heat. Add in the diced sweet potatoes and season with cumin, paprika, chili powder, garlic powder and salt. Cook until the potatoes are soft (about 10 minutes). Then add in the drained black beans and cook for another 2-3 minutes until everything is heated through.

To assemble the tacos grab 8-10 tortillas (or however many you like) spread some of the mixture on each taco shell then top with your favorite toppings like shredded cheese, tomatoes, lettuce, or salsa. Enjoy!

These vegetarian tacos are a great way to get your kids eating healthier and trying new vegetarian recipes. They're easy to make, full of flavor, and customizable with whatever toppings you have on hand. Give these vegetarian black bean and sweet potato tacos a try for your next vegetarian dinner! Your family will love them.

Vegetarian Chilli Mac

Ingredients

1 tablespoon olive oil.
1 cup chopped onion.
1 bell pepper (chopped small, any color)
2 medium carrots (chopped into ¼-inch pieces)
3 cloves garlic (minced)
1 tablespoon chili powder.
1 ½ teaspoons ground cumin.

Vegetarian chilli mac is an easy, healthy vegetarian recipe that can be enjoyed by kids of all ages. With simple ingredients like onions, bell peppers, carrots and garlic, this dish packs in plenty of flavor and nutrition. To prepare vegetarian chilli mac, start by heating the olive oil in a large pot over medium-high heat. Add the chopped onion and sauté for two minutes until softened. Then add the bell pepper, carrots and garlic to the pot and cook for three more minutes until vegetables are softened. Next, stir in chili powder, cumin and salt; reduce heat to low and simmer for five minutes more. Finally, serve vegetarian chilli mac with your favorite toppings such as shredded cheese or sour cream! This vegetarian recipe is a perfect way to get your kids to eat their veggies and enjoy the flavors of a delicious meal. With vegetarian chilli mac, you can rest assured that your family is eating healthy and enjoying every bite!

Tofu Sandwich

Are you looking for vegetarian recipes for kids? Then look no further than this delicious tofu sandwich. It's a healthy and easy meal that your children will adore. Start by toasting some of their favorite bread, and spread with Thousand Island dressing. To make the sandwich extra special, add lettuce, tomatoes, avocado, cucumber and sprouts. This vegetarian recipe is sure to please everyone in the family! To prepare it, simply assemble all of the ingredients into the sandwich and serve. Your kids will love it! Enjoy!

The tofu sandwich is a great vegetarian alternative for kids and makes a healthy, easy meal that can be prepared quickly. A delicious combination of toasted bread, Thousand Island dressing, lettuce, tomatoes, avocado, cucumber and sprouts makes this vegetarian recipe both nutritious and tasty. It's an ideal way to get your kids to enjoy vegetarian meals - just assemble the ingredients into the sandwich and serve! Your children will love it and you can feel good knowing they are getting their daily dose of veggies. Kids need all the nutrition they can get - so why not try this vegetarian recipe today? Enjoy!

Black Bean Quinoa Tacos

Ingredients

2 tablespoons oil.
½ red onion diced.
1 jalapeño diced.
¾ cup quinoa dry.
1 15-ounce can black beans drained and rinsed.
2 tablespoons taco seasoning.
1 ½ cups broth or water.

If you're looking for vegetarian recipes for kids that are both healthy and delicious, look no further than this black bean quinoa taco recipe. This kid-approved vegetarian dish is simple to make and packed with flavor. Plus, it only takes about 30 minutes of prep time before it's ready to serve.

To start preparing this vegetarian recipe for kids, heat 2 tablespoons of oil in a large skillet over medium-high heat. Then add the diced onion and jalapeno and cook until tender, about 5 minutes. Once done, add the dry quinoa to the pan and stir until evenly coated with oil. Next, add the beans, taco seasoning and broth or water to the skillet and mix together. Bring to a low boil and reduce to a simmer, then cook until the quinoa is tender, about 15 minutes.

Once done, you're ready to assemble your black bean quinoa tacos. Serve with warm tortillas and your favorite taco toppings. Then enjoy this vegetarian meal that the entire family can love!

This vegetarian recipe for kids is sure to become a regular in your household, thanks to its delicious flavor and healthy ingredients. Plus, it only requires minimal prep time so you can easily prepare it on busy nights. Try out this vegetarian recipe for kids today and enjoy!

Vegan Mac And Cheese

Vegan mac and cheese is a vegetarian-friendly take on the classic dish that kids love. It's an easy, healthy recipe that can be quickly prepared any night of the week. To make vegan mac and cheese, you'll need 1 1/2 cups raw cashews, 2 cups water, 3 tablespoons fresh lemon juice, 1/2 cup nutritional yeast, 1/4 teaspoon turmeric, 1/2 teaspoon garlic powder and 1 1/2 teaspoons salt. For vegetarian recipes for kids, you can also add a 7-oz bag of shredded vegan cheddar cheese for extra flavor.

To prepare your vegan mac and cheese: first combine the cashews with the water in a blender or food processor until smooth. Next add the lemon juice, nutritional yeast, turmeric, garlic powder and salt. Blend until creamy and smooth.

Pour the mixture into a pot and cook over medium-high heat while stirring constantly. Once the sauce has thickened, remove it from heat and stir in the shredded cheese if using. Serve warm with your favorite vegetarian sides like steamed broccoli or edamame beans.

Vegan mac and cheese makes for a healthy recipe that kids will love as an alternative to traditional macaroni dishes. Enjoy!

Vegan Enchiladas

These vegetarian black bean enchiladas are a great way to get your kids involved in making dinner! Not only will they have fun helping you prepare this healthy recipe, but they'll love the delicious Mexican flavors.

To make these vegetarian black bean enchiladas, you'll need black beans (either canned or cooked from dry beans), garlic, onion, chili powder and cumin for a traditional Mexican flavor, sea salt to bring all the flavors together, and fresh cilantro.

Once you've gathered your ingredients, it's time to start cooking. Begin by sautéing the garlic and onion in some oil until softened. Now add the black beans along with the chili powder and cumin - mix everything together and cook for a few minutes to let the flavors combine.

When your black bean filling is ready, it's time to assemble the enchiladas. Place some of the bean mixture in each tortilla, top with fresh cilantro, and roll up into a cylinder shape. Place these vegetarian enchiladas in a baking dish, pour on some enchilada sauce and cover with cheese (optional). Bake until heated through and bubbly.

Serve these vegetarian black bean enchiladas with your favorite sides for a delicious vegetarian meal that even picky eaters will love! You can also freeze any leftovers for quick meals down the road. With this healthy vegetarian recipe, you'll be serving up happy meals in no time. Enjoy!

Vegetarian Burger

Ingredients

1 x 400 g tin of chickpeas.
1 x 340 g tin of sweetcorn.
½ a bunch of fresh coriander , (15g)
½ teaspoon paprika.
½ teaspoon ground coriander.
½ teaspoon ground cumin.
1 lemon.
3 heaped tablespoons plain flour , plus extra for dusting.!

If you're looking for vegetarian recipes that are fun and healthy for kids, look no further than this vegetarian burger! This delicious vegetarian dish is easy to prepare and packed with flavour. With a combination of tinned chickpeas, sweetcorn, fresh herbs, spices and a squeeze of lemon juice, these vegetarian burgers are sure to please even the pickiest eaters.

To make the vegetarian burgers, start by draining and rinsing the chickpeas before placing them in a bowl. Add the sweetcorn and finely chopped coriander leaves. Mix together all of the spices - paprika, ground coriander, ground cumin - before adding them to the bowl along with a squeeze of lemon juice. Give it all a good mix before adding the plain flour to help bind it together.

Shape the vegetarian burger mixture into balls, then flatten them out into patties and lightly dust with flour before frying in a pan for around 3 minutes each side until golden brown and crisp. Serve your vegetarian burgers hot with your favourite accompaniments - from salad leaves to mashed potato! Enjoy!

Cashew Alfredo Sauce

INGREDIENTS

1 1/4 CUPS RAW CASHEWS
(SOAKED)
1 TBSP ARROWROOT STARCH
(OPTIONAL)
3-4 TBSP NUTRITIONAL YEAST.
2-3 CLOVES GARLIC* (CRUSHED)
1-2 TBSP VEGAN PARMESAN
CHEESE (PLUS MORE FOR SERVING)
1-2 CUPS UNSWEETENED PLAIN
ALMOND OR RICE MILK (PLUS MORE
AS NEEDED)

Alfredo Cashew Alfredo Sauce is a delicious vegetarian option for kids that's both healthy and easy to prepare. To make the sauce, simply soak 1 1/4 cups of raw cashews overnight and then blend with a few simple ingredients such as arrowroot starch (optional), nutritional yeast, crushed garlic, vegan parmesan cheese, almond or rice milk. Depending on desired consistency and flavor, adjust the amount of each ingredient accordingly. The final product should be smooth and creamy!

To serve this sauce over pasta or vegetables, start by bringing a pot of salted water to boil. Add your favorite vegetarian-friendly noodles or veggies and cook until tender. Once finished cooking, drain the contents in a colander and return to the pot. Pour in your Alfredo Cashew Alfredo Sauce, stirring gently until the desired consistency is achieved. Sprinkle with vegan parmesan cheese, and serve hot for a delicious vegetarian dinner that kids will love!

For an even heartier dish, add some sautéed mushrooms or asparagus to the mix! With its creamy texture and savory flavor, this Alfredo sauce is sure to become a family favorite. Enjoy!

Black Bean Burger

Creating vegetarian recipes for kids can be easy and healthy with the help of a black bean burger. This vegetarian meal is packed full of protein, fiber, and other essential nutrients to keep your little ones healthy and strong. Here's how to prepare it:

Ingredients:
- 1 (15 ounce) can black beans, drained and rinsed
- 3 baby carrots, grated (Optional)
- ⅓ cup chopped sweet onion.
- ¼ cup minced green bell pepper (Optional)
- 1 tablespoon minced garlic.
- 3 tablespoons chile-garlic sauce (such as Sriracha®), or to taste
- 1 tablespoon cornstarch.
- 1 tablespoon warm water.

Instructions:
1. In a medium bowl, mash the black beans with a fork until they are mostly broken up but still chunky.
2. Add the grated carrots, sweet onion, bell pepper, garlic and chile-garlic sauce and mix together with the mashed beans until everything is evenly combined.
3. In a small bowl, mix together the cornstarch and warm water until it forms a paste and then add it to the bean mixture and mix again until everything is completely integrated.
4. Heat a skillet over medium heat and shape the bean mixture into four patties about ¾ inch thick each. Place them in the skillet and cook for 4 minutes on each side or until golden brown.
5. Serve the black bean burgers with your favorite condiments and a side of fresh vegetables for a healthy vegetarian meal your kids will love!

Enjoy!

Vegetarian Egg Muffins

Vegetarian egg muffins are a great way to get your kids excited about vegetarian recipes. Not only are they healthy and delicious, but they're so easy to prepare! All you need is a few simple ingredients, some basic kitchen tools, and you can have vegetarian egg muffins ready in no time. To begin, gather the ingredients - 3 cups of mixed vegetables (such as broccoli, mushrooms, peppers, and spinach), 1 teaspoon oil, 12 large eggs, ¼ cup milk, ½ teaspoon black pepper & salt to taste, ½ teaspoon dry mustard powder, 3 tablespoons onion minced and 1 cup cheddar cheese.

In a large bowl whisk together the eggs with the milk until well combined. Add the seasonings with the oil and then add in the vegetables, onion, and cheese. Mix everything together until all ingredients are evenly distributed.

Using a muffin tin lined with paper liners or sprayed with non-stick cooking spray, evenly spoon the vegetarian egg mixture into each cup. Bake in preheated oven for about 20 minutes, or until egg muffins are cooked through.

Once cooked, vegetarian egg muffins can be served warm or cold and make excellent snacks for kids. They are a great grab-and-go option for lunchboxes and after school snacks that your kids will love! With just a few simple ingredients and minimal preparation, vegetarian egg muffins are a healthy and delicious option for kids. Try them today and let your kids enjoy the vegetarian recipes!

Breakfast Pear Crisp

This vegetarian breakfast pear crisp is a great way to get your kids involved in making healthy recipes. It's easy to prepare and full of delicious, nutritious ingredients that will leave them feeling satisfied.

To make it, you'll need 2 big pears (or alternatively 2 3/4 cups of diced pears). Then mix ½ tablespoon of cornstarch, 1 ½ tablespoons of maple syrup and the juice from one orange in a bowl. Add this mixture to the pears and set aside.

In a separate bowl, mix together 1 cup of rolled oats, ¼ cup of flour, 1 ½ tablespoons of brown sugar and 1 teaspoon cinnamon. Then stir in the pear mixture and pour into a 9x13 baking dish.

Pop the dish into the oven and bake at 350°F for 25 minutes, or until golden brown on top. Serve warm with a scoop of ice cream and enjoy!

This vegetarian breakfast pear crisp is sure to become a family favorite. Not only is it quick and easy to make, it's also healthy and vegetarian-friendly. Get the kids involved in the preparation process to make a fun family activity out of it! With this delicious pear crisp, you can be sure that your family will have a nutritious start to the day.

Egg On Avocado Toast

Avocado toast is a delicious, vegetarian-friendly and healthy meal for kids. Preparing it is simple and doesn't require many ingredients. Here's how you can make an egg on avocado toast recipe:

To start, you'll need one slice of whole grain or gluten-free bread that has been toasted. I recommend Dave's Killer Bread Good Seed Thin Sliced for the perfect texture and flavor. After toasting, spread a thin layer of mashed avocado (about one ounce from a quarter of a small haas avocado) onto the bread.

Next, spray cooking oil into a pan and crack an egg in the center. Cook until the egg whites are set and the yolk is still runny. Season with salt and pepper to taste, then carefully slide onto the avocado toast.

Optionally, you can add a few hot sauce or red pepper flakes for an extra kick of flavor. Serve immediately and enjoy this vegetarian-friendly egg on avocado toast recipe!

Kids will love this delicious, healthy and vegetarian-friendly meal. With a few simple steps, they can enjoy this tasty breakfast or lunch with minimal effort. Egg on avocado toast is the perfect dish for busy mornings and afternoons!

Happy cooking!

Vegan French Toast

Vegan French Toast is a vegetarian-friendly recipe perfect for kids. All you need is some sliced bread of choice, a banana (or coconut cream or flax eggs for a vegan version), nondairy milk, sweetener, and a pinch of salt. For added flavor, sprinkle on some optional nutritional yeast and cinnamon.

To prepare the vegan French toast, start by mashing the banana in a bowl until smooth. Alternatively, you can mix together coconut cream or flax eggs to achieve a similar consistency. Next, add the nondairy milk and sweetener, stirring together until combined. Finally, season with a pinch of salt and stir in optional nutritional yeast and cinnamon for extra flavor.

Once the French toast batter is ready, dip the slices of bread into the mixture and let it sit for a few minutes before cooking on a greased skillet over medium heat. Flip when golden brown and cook until both sides are evenly browned. Serve with your favorite toppings, such as vegan butter, syrup or fresh berries!

No Egg Pancakes

Making vegetarian-friendly no egg pancakes is a quick, easy and healthy way to appeal to your kids' taste buds. This recipe can be easily adapted for vegetarian diets and there are only a few simple ingredients needed to make it. Here's how you can prepare vegetarian no egg pancakes in just a few minutes:

Ingredients:
- 1 1/4 cups all-purpose flour
- 1 tablespoon baking powder
- 1 tablespoon sugar
- 1/4 teaspoon salt
- 1 cup non-fat or 1% milk
- 2 tablespoons vegetable oil
- 2 tablespoons water

Instructions:
1. In a large bowl, combine the flour, baking powder, sugar and salt.

2. In a separate bowl, mix together the milk, vegetable oil and water until it forms a thick paste.

3. Slowly pour the liquid ingredients into the dry ones while mixing with a whisk or fork until you have a batter without any lumps.

4. Heat a non-stick pan over medium heat and grease it lightly with vegetable oil.

5. Drop one tablespoon of the batter into the center of the pan at a time and spread it evenly to form small pancakes. Cook each side for about 1-2 minutes or until golden brown.

6. Serve vegetarian no egg pancakes with your favorite toppings such as butter, honey or syrup.

Making vegetarian no egg pancakes is an easy way to add a healthy and delicious meal to your child's diet. It's sure to be a hit with the whole family! Enjoy!

Vegan Mashed Potatoes

Vegan mashed potatoes are a delicious and healthy vegetarian recipe that's perfect for kids. With this simple recipe, you can easily prepare vegan mashed potatoes that your family is sure to love!

To get started, simply wash and scrub 6-8 medium yukon gold potatoes (if large, cut in half) and add them to a pot. Cover the potatoes with water, add 1/2 tsp of sea salt, and bring to a boil. Boil the potatoes until they are tender, about 15-20 minutes.

Once the potatoes are cooked, drain them and mash them using your favorite method. We prefer a potato masher or an electric mixer for best results. Once mashed, add 1/2 tsp of ground black pepper and 5-6 cloves of raw or roasted garlic (or sub minced garlic sautéed for 3 minutes in olive oil). Gently mix the ingredients until fully incorporated and then add 3-4 tablespoons of vegan butter (such as Earth Balance) to give it a creamy texture.

Season to taste, and you're done! Serve your vegan mashed potatoes hot with a sprinkle of salt and pepper. Your family will love this vegetarian recipe that's both healthy and delicious! Enjoy!

Vegan Creamy Cucumber Salad

This vegan creamy cucumber salad is a delicious vegetarian recipe that kids will love! It's easy to prepare and full of healthy ingredients - perfect for lunch boxes or after-school snacks. To make it, you'll need 2/3 cup finely diced red onion (or halved & thinly sliced with a mandolin* // ~1/2 medium onion as recipe is written), 1 large clove garlic, minced, 1 cup unsweetened plain coconut yogurt (we like Culina), 1/2 tsp each sea salt and black pepper and 2 Tbsp lemon juice (~1 medium lemon as recipe is written).

To prepare the salad, start by combining the diced red onion with the minced garlic and lemon juice in a bowl. Mix until the ingredients are well-combined, then add the coconut yogurt, salt and pepper. Stir until everything is evenly mixed together. Finally, fold in the cucumber slices until they are evenly covered with the dressing. Serve chilled or at room temperature and enjoy!

This vegan creamy cucumber salad is a great vegetarian recipe for kids. It's healthy, flavorful and easy to prepare - perfect for lunch boxes or after-school snacks! And best of all, it will make sure your children are getting the nutrients they need. Enjoy!

Spinach Tomato Quesadillas

Preparing vegetarian recipes for kids doesn't have to be complicated or time consuming. These vegetarian spinach tomato quesadillas are easy to make, healthy and tasty!

To get started making these vegetarian spinach tomato quesadillas you will need the following ingredients: 1 roma tomato (thinly sliced), 3/4 cup fresh baby spinach, 1/4 cup vegan pesto, 1/2 cup vegan mozzarella shreds, 1/4 cup vegan feta crumbles (optional), and 2 large tortillas.

To begin your vegetarian recipe for kids, preheat a large skillet on medium heat. Place one of the tortillas in the preheated skillet and layer with half of the pesto, tomato slices, spinach, mozzarella shreds and feta crumbles if desired. Top with the remaining tortilla, pressing gently to ensure it sticks together.

Cook for 1-2 minutes on each side until golden brown and the cheese is melted. Slice into 4 wedges, serve and enjoy!

These vegetarian spinach tomato quesadillas make a great lunch or snack for kids that is both healthy and delicious. Enjoy!

Beetroot Pasta

This vegetarian beetroot pasta recipe is healthy and easy to prepare, making it perfect for kids! To get started, preheat your oven to 200°C (400°F). Place the chopped beetroot on a baking tray lined with parchment paper and drizzle with olive oil. Roast in the preheated oven for about 15 minutes until soft.

Meanwhile, heat the remaining oil in a large pan and fry the onions, celery, carrots, basil and garlic over a medium-high heat for about 10 minutes until softened. Once the vegetables are cooked through, add in the roasted beetroot chunks and stir to combine.

Add the pasta to a pot of boiling, salted water and cook according to the instructions on the packet. Once cooked, drain and add to the pan with the vegetables and beetroot. Mix everything together, season with salt and freshly ground black pepper to taste, then serve.

This vegetarian beetroot pasta is a great choice for kids' lunchboxes or as an easy weeknight dinner. It also works well as a vegetarian alternative for family gatherings or parties. Enjoy!

Thank you

We hope you enjoyed our book.

As a small family company ,your feedback is very important to us.

Please let us know how you like your book